Seven Rs

TO YOUR SUCCESS AND DESTINY

Tarupiwa Muzah

Contents

CHAPTER 1

REASON [WHY DO IT]

You must find the reason, so that you know the season. Reasons move you, they energize you. You must know why you are doing something first, so that you build a solid foundation.

To find the reason why is to find your drive, or what drives you. Why do you want it done? Are you doing it for fun or do you want something out of it?

You must know your inmost values; what do you cherish? These will kick-start the process to your destiny. What is your inner satisfaction; know it and you will discover your motivation.

Involve God in your search, pray for him to reveal His will for you. The will of God is what he wants out of you, what he has purposed for you; this becomes your reason why you do that. Reasons make you strong. You then say I'm doing this because it brings God pleasure when I do it. He has ordained it for me.

Colossians 4 verse 12- Always laboring fervently for you in prayers that ye may stand perfect and complete in all the will of God.

Those who know God's will become unstoppable. They have a reason to do what they do; they say, because God said do it, I will do it.

Be it in business, in your work, or career, why are you doing that? Do you want to make millions, or to help people? Know your reason; it becomes the push factor in your destiny pursuit.

Some reasons you think on your own, but you can also get insight from the word of God.

1 Thessalonians 4 verse 11-12- And that you study to be quiet, and to do your own business, and to work with your own hands, as we commanded you. Verse 12 speaks of the reasons why, that ye may walk honestly toward them that are without, and that ye may have lack of nothing.

A reason defines your principles, controls your conduct and shows your aim of doing something. You say I'm doing this because I'm escaping the corruption that is in the world through lust. I'm doing honest service, and I want to lack nothing, I want to be fully provided for.

Verse 12 [NIV version], so that your daily life may win the respect of outsiders, and so that you will not be dependent on anybody.

This will move you to act. You say I don't want to be dependent on anybody; I want to be respected and honored. That's why I'm doing this.

1 Timothy 6 verse 18-19- That they do good, that they be rich in good works, ready to distribute, willing to communicate. Verse 19 speaks of the reason why, laying up in store for themselves a good foundation against the time to come, that they may lay hold on eternal life.

Reasons give you peace of mind, now you say I'm doing this business, ministry, work because I'm laying a good foundation for the time to come, and these deeds are preparing me for eternity, they are eternal.

1 Timothy 4 verse 14-15- Do not neglect your gift, which was given you through a prophetic message when the body of elders laid their hands on you. Verse 15 speaks of the reason why. Be diligent in these

matters; give yourself wholly to them, so that everyone may see your progress.

Reasons keep you from being passive. Now you say I will use my gifting; give myself diligently to it. Why? Because I want everyone to see my progress. The other version says, so that thy profiting may appear to all,,you say I want everyone to see that I'm profiting from this gift, business or work.

CHAPTER 2

RESEARCH [HOW TO DO IT]

Information is success and also power. Don't just go blindfolded. Find out how to do it, and you will enter your destiny.

Research leads to insight, it leads to a switch on of a light in the dark corner of your mind. You get many surprises as you search. It quickens you to act, because you will get knowledge on the steps to take.

Instead of wondering, go for information gathering. You are what you know, and what you know is what you are.

You are secure if you do it the way that it's supposed to be done, and you will be successful. Find the correct way to do it, by research. You hit your target when you have the know-how.

Wisdom is application; it's the how to of any given endeavor. Get counsel before you wage your war.

Research helps you in your planning process. To be good in planning, have information first; be advised by those who are knowledgeable about your quest.

Proverbs 20 verse 18- Make plans by seeking advice; if you wage war, obtain guidance.

Be it in business, ministry, your gifting or work, you need to plan and set goals with deadlines. To do this, you need info. Learn from the best and learn from others. Learn from the founding fathers.

Be filled with the Spirit. He is the spirit of counsel, he is the greatest researcher. He searches the deep things of the heart of God, and reveals it to you. He makes you to understand your gift, and gives you insight on how to use it.

1 John 2 verse 27- But the anointing which ye have received of him abideth in you, and ye need not that any man teach you; but as the same anointing teacheth you of all things, and is truth, and is no lie.

Don't get research from one source, be broad, get as many sources as possible, and you will make it. You will reach your destiny. Compare and contrast the info, then use what best suits you.

Proverbs 15 verse 22- Without counsel purposes are disappointed; but in the multitude of counselors they are established.

The establishment comes with the multitude of sources; don't be lazy to read, to study and to discover more about what you want to do.

Research makes you ready, ready to do it. It gives you an anticipation, because its preparation. You are getting charged as you get first hand information of how it can be done.

You are removing doubt. When you know how, doubt ceases to exist.

CHAPTER 3

RESVRCES [THE MEANS TO DO IT]

Use the resources that are there, don't wait for bigger things, start from the little that you have. Look at what you have. You have time, it's a resource, use it well.

Value time and you will increase your value. Invest in it; it will earn you a brighter future. Your destiny is contained in time management.

Resources are assets and instruments of change; they enhance your dreams and enlarge your possibilities.

Everything you dream becomes possible when you got the resources to use to reach there.

God said to Moses, "What do you have in your hand? Use it." No one can say, "I have nothing." The little you have can catapult you to your destiny.

Someone once said poverty is lack of motivation to use the resources that are there. But I say its lack of the eyes to see what you have with you.

What's your focus? What do you see? Don't look at what you don't have, look at what you have and you will succeed. When you focus on what's lacking, you will become stagnant, you will not move. You will say I'm waiting to have this or that so that I can do it.

John 6 verse 9- There is a lad here, which hath five barley loaves, and two small fishes, but what are they among so many?

The question was a doubt, but Jesus was quick to see that it's enough for all; he knew that from that little seed, a miracle would happen. You see what you want to see when you look at your resources; some see addition, some multiplication, and some subtraction.

Someone saw the moon in the sky, and said, this is a resource, and did not see any addition, but when someone else saw it, he saw satellites, the multiplication of information sharing, and now we have the television.

David slayed the head of Goliath with only five smooth stones. He used what he had. Be positive, always, and you will soon see that you have the means to an end.

Proverbs 14 verse 4- Where no oxen are, the crib is clean; but much increase is by the strength of the ox.

Resources lead to much increase, when you have them, abundance will be the result.

Resources start as a seed and ends as a harvest. They are both tangible and intangible. Ideas are resources too, because without them no product will come to be.

Nature your ideas, they will lead you to your accumulation. They are a means to an end.

CHAPTER 4

RISK [JUST DO IT]

Outstanding effort is about taking risks. Measure your effort in any undertaking, and see if it's low or high. When your effort is high, it means you are risking more, and doing more.

A champion will always have the greatest commitment and energy in carrying out assignments.

Don't hesitate to do it, or seem like you don't even want to do it. No, RISE, just do it. Don't leave your dreams on paper. No, walk into them; step by step. Your destiny is fulfilled by action.

Proverbs 14 verse 23- All hard work brings a profit, but mere talk leads only to poverty.

Your talk must correspond with your walk. Don't just talk about it, do it, and you will see yourself become it. When you talk big, you must also do big.

You cannot underestimate the value of a little action because it will lead to perfection. You develop your craft as you act on it.

Shun all excuses of not acting, they hinder your progress. Don't wait for conditions to be favorable for you to act, or you will be waiting forever. Do it anyhow, do it in contradiction, do it in conflict, and do it even when misunderstood. You will make it to the other side.

Proverbs 20 verse 4- The sluggard will not plow by reason of the cold; therefore shall he beg in harvest, and have nothing.

The situation may be cold for you, but don't stop acting on your dream, gifting, business or ministry. You will soon see a change.

Test and see that the Lord is good. You may have great faith but you haven't put it to the test. You may have great ability but haven't yet pushed it to the limit, so that you see.

Put it out there, your idea, test it, and see. Let the customers decide, you might be the next big thing, but you won't know it, if you don't test it.

Someone once said, "Don't worry, be happy!" But I say, "Don't worry, be active." Do something and you will be something, and what you fret about will evaporate into thin air.

Malachi 3 verse 10- Test me in this, says the Lord Almighty, and see if I will not throw open the floodgates of heaven and pour out so much blessing that you will not have room enough for it.

Yes, just test and you will see, give it out, and you will see the blessing of the Lord. You will be successful and you will enter your destiny.

They say high risk, high return. When the risk is too much, the profit of the venture is also too much. To risk is to take a chance on something. So do it, the chances are that you might make it, you might win.

CHAPTER 5

RESILIENCE [TO DO IT AGAIN]

To bounce back from defeat is the essence of greatness. It is when you don't accept no for an answer. You are a winner if you possess this attitude.

Spring back into the action gear, and hold your head up again, you might make it with just another blow. Try again on that relationship, on that business or ministry; you will be rewarded for your resilience.

Be unbreakable as you pursue your destiny. You need that tenacity; it will do you good in the face of major setbacks.

From a setback to a comeback is what you are destined for, you must be restored to your former state of glory, and be even better than before.

That failure is not final; it's just a stepping stone to greater victory. It's about your interpretation of what has happened. Do it again, and know that you are in a process of success.

What you want also wants you; it's yours for the taking. Come back to it, do it now in another way. Improve in the way you do it. You will surely enter your destiny.

That project that you left hanging, saying it's not profitable, go back to it again, and revisit it with much eagerness to perfect it. It wasn't that bad. You will find out that you just lost the drive to continue developing it.

Proverbs 19 verse 24- The sluggard buries his hand in the dish; he will not even bring it back to his mouth.

Resilience is a quality of the diligent. They bring things back to life. So don't bury your gift, your talent, or your passion; work hard and bring it back to its prominence.

They are many things you have buried because you were not willing to cultivate them. Start afresh, revisit that business, that ministry and now water it, give it the needed nutrients for growth.

Our savior Jesus Christ, the Epitome of resilience, he died, and on the third day, he came back to life again. And by his blood we are now forgiven of all our sins, and we are now blessed children of God.

It seemed like failure to die, but that failure was not final, he bounced back from it into glory, the death's sting became history.

CHAPTER 6

RELATION [GET HELP TO DO IT]

To relate is to reduce the load, it is to ease the burden, and to be rest assured of success and destiny. This is because you have put it in safe hands.

Now get others involved, that's a big step to success. The familiar of business is that you are the boss, and also do your own marketing, accounting and management. Now relation means to do it in a different way. Get into contractual agreements with others to help you in all that.

To relate is to empower others in your destiny exploits. It leads to fast wins, because experts are now part of the things you do.

Professional help is the sparkplug to real development and production. You were doing it alone, but see, you haven't really gone that far. But see how far you will go if you get those qualified and experienced in doing it involved.

You can do it more than those who studied for it. Yes you can, but in rare occasions. Change the way you do things, and things will change and get done. Try what you have never tried, and you will go where you have never gone.

Matthew 7 verse 7- Ask and it will be given; seek and you will find; knock and the door will be opened.

Did you ever seek that professional help? You haven't tried, now seek it and surely, you will find it. Have you ever knocked on the doors of companies? You have not, do it; knock and the door will be opened.

Your idea needs backing, that's the thing that is lacking.

Enter into partnership agreements with those with the skills, and you will see the benefits. It's about interaction, know how to network and relate well with people.

Never think it's unnecessary, because those who are qualified have in-depth information, and the ability to tackle any given situation which relates to that field.

Your desire must match with the actions you are willing to take. You want greatness, you want to make it big, but look at your relations. You are doing it all, and that's small. You only know a little about marketing, distribution, and about sales. How do you expect to reach greater heights with that little information?

Stretch yourself, be flexible, allow yourself to get help to do it. Get those professionals involved by offering them a percentage of the profit, and you will reach to the top you desire.

CHAPTER 7

REWARD [REAP BENEFITS OF DOING IT]

Rewards are what you gain from doing it. They come after service. Rewards are the results of following principles. Because of your hard work, now you reap the benefits.

When you were doing it, you were planting, and after planting, there comes the harvest. The harvest is the reward of having done something.

1 Corinthians 9 verse 7-10- Who serves as a soldier at his own expense? Who plants a vineyard and does not eat of its grapes? Who tends a flock and does not drink of the milk? Do I say this merely from a human point

of view? Doesn't the law say the same thing? For it is written in the law of Moses, Do not muzzle an ox while it is treading out the grain, is it about oxen that God is concerned? Surely he says this for us, doesn't he? Yes, this was written for us, because when the plowman plows and the thresher threshes, they ought to do so in the hope of sharing in the harvest.

You have a right to reap the benefits of your labor. It's God's will for you to enjoy the harvest of your sowing. God is concerned about you; he sees your work and rewards you accordingly. He also said seed time and harvest shall not cease.

Success is when you succeed successfully.

There are laws of success and you have obeyed them, now you get what you deserve. Hard work is one of the laws. The best in giving becomes the best in receiving.

Learn the art of receiving, expect your rewards, command your value, and take what you need, all of it.

Psalms 128 verse 2- For thou shalt eat the labour of thine hands; happy shalt thou be, and it shall be well with thee.

Rewards come after labour. It's a promise of God that you shall enjoy, so say yes to it, and it will be fulfilled in your life.

When you get rewards, you know it's time for celebration, you have made it, and you are blessed. You have given, and a good measure has been given back to you. God is faithful and true to his word.

You are now being treated in a special way because you have obeyed. You will be satisfied with the results of your actions; you will eat in plenty and be satisfied. You went through thick and thin to reach to the place called there. It's a place of victory, where you now get the benefits of your toil and travail.

Isaiah 53 verse 11- He shall see of the travail of his soul, and shall be satisfied; by his knowledge shall my righteous servant justify many; for he shall bear their iniquities.

This is our Lord and saviour Jesus Christ. Yes, he did it; he went through it, and he gave himself. He suffered and he was resilient, he bounced back, he died and rose again on the third day. Now by his blood, he justifies many. He says not guilty to many, he declares them righteous. He shall see the reward of his action, his labour and be satisfied.

He is now reaping the harvest of his plantation as millions of people are being saved from their sins, and becoming blessed through him. Many are having life eternal through his sacrifice.

They believe in him, that he did it for them. He is now reaping the benefits of doing it. He did not just do it for nothing. No; the action was a seed, leading to a great harvest of souls.

Many now enter the kingdom of God because of his action. Many are receiving the promise of the Holy Spirit; they are being empowered for great things. Only because of what he did, he is now impacting many generations.

Notes

Notes

37

www.ingramcontent.com/pod-product-compliance
Lightning Source LLC
Chambersburg PA
CBHW061103050726

47592CB00004B/1813